T0359588

Spotto

The Great Australian Car Game

Spotty McSpotterson

Woodslane Press Pty Ltd
10 Apollo Street
Warriewood, NSW 2102
Email: info@woodslane.com.au
Website: www.woodslanepress.com.au
Tel: 02 8445 2300

First published in Australia in 2024 by Woodslane Press
© 2024 Woodslane Press, text and images © 2024

The information in this publication is based upon the current state of w and industry practice and the general
circumstances as at the date of publication. Every effort has been made to obtain permissions relating to
information reproduced in this publication. The publisher makes no representations as to the accuracy,
reliability or completeness of the information contained in this publication. To the extent permitted by law, the
publisher excludes all conditions, warranties and other obligations in relation to the supply of this publication
and otherwise limits its liability to the recommended retail price. In no circumstances will the publisher
be liable to any third party for any consequential loss or damage suffered by any person resulting in any
way from the use or reliance on this publication or any part of it. Any opinions and advice contained in the
publication are offered solely in pursuance of the author's and publisher's intention to provide information
and have not been specifically sought.

A catalogue record for this
book is available from the
National Library of Australia

NATIONAL LIBRARY OF AUSTRALIA

FSC
www.fsc.org
MIX
Supporting
responsible forestry
FSC® C151165

Printed in China by Jilin GIGO
Cover image by Cory Spence
Book design by Cory Spence

Disclaimer: Drive safely at all times.
The materials presented in this book are distributed by the
Author for and on behalf of Spotto players and enthusiasts
as an inspiration source only. The Author; makes no
statements, representations or warranties about the
accuracy or completeness of, and you should not rely on,
any information contained in this book.
The Author disclaims all responsibility and all liability
(including without limitation, liability in negligence) for
all expenses, losses, damages, arguments, relationship
breakups, hurt feelings, melted snowflakes and costs which
you might incur as a result of the information contained
in this book being inaccurate or incomplete in any way.
The Author makes no warranties that this book is free of
viruses, ghosts, alien infections, parallel universes, cryptid
astrology or other contamination. The Author recommends
that you use appropriate investigation and research befor
acting upon any information from this book.

contents

> **Some painters transform the sun into a yellow spot, others transform a yellow spot into the sun.**
>
> – Pablo Picasso

prologue

The game is ours

This is *NOT* a rule book. There *IS* no rule book. This is a philosophical reference guide intended to explore the nuances and details in the great Australian game of Spotto. Think of it more as a spiritual companion in your journey to yellow enlightenment.

Throughout the next few chapters you will find your intellect challenged as the concepts are laid out and YOU, the reader, is asked to provide the definitions of the game inside your own vehicle.

With so many overlapping and internally referential concepts, it is recommended that this discourse be consumed in a single sitting.
Local rules apply –
always.

auth**o**r

The elusive professor

Professor McSpotterson, the elusive wordsmith of the yellow automobile jungle, is renowned for his ability to vanish around a street corner just when you thought you had a chance to see him. Rumour has it that he holds secret seminars from behind a yellow desk in a yellow-painted office.

Spotty grew up in the school of hard spots and earned multiple degrees in Applied Spotting Science before completing a PhD with his first academic paper *Spectral Yellology: A Theoretical Framework for the Observational Dynamics of Spontaneous Yellow Car Spotting in Urban Environments*. This paper has come to be known as the "Great Bananalysis"

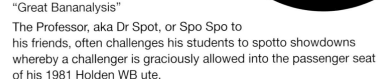

The Professor, aka Dr Spot, or Spo Spo to his friends, often challenges his students to spotto showdowns whereby a challenger is graciously allowed into the passenger seat of his 1981 Holden WB ute.

Rumour states the Professor acquired his superhuman skills when he frolicked in a field of sunflowers as a child and was stung on the bridge of his nose by a *Vespula pensylvanica*.

hello

It's all up to you

Welcome to the first and only Spotto book that is a fully comprehensive guide to the much loved game of Spotto. Even though we have all played it on many a road trip or still do, do we really know or understand the foundations and history of this game? We will cover eveything from science to spottosophy to history so that you can become enlightened within the entire spotto universe. Lucky for you, I am here to help you through this processs. This book will cover topics in the following chapters to allow all of us to share in the knowledge and answer the big questions:

- When do *YOU* enter the game?
- When does a vehicle become spottable?
- Can you split a trip?
- What *IS* yellow?

The game requires players to firstly understand the strict boundary conditions that surround concepts of these questions which in turn allows us to define the parameters of the local rules e.g. we must first rigorously, definitely and precisely agree on this – **only then may the game proceed.**

Left: One set of rules for the whole world; Right: Local rules for each car.

Perception

Reality

6

Cargument [**cahr**·gyuh·muhnt]
noun

1. An oral disagreement; verbal opposition; contention; altercation inside a vehicle, usually a car.

2. An angry quarrel or disagreement involving different point of view while travelling in a car.

   We had a cargument about Spotto

Carticipant [cahr-**tis**-uh-puhnt]
noun

1. A person joining in a car game.

adjective

2. Carticipating; sharing in the car game.

Spotto [spot-oh]
noun

1. The name of the game.

   Let's play a game of Spotto.

interjection, exclamation

2. Announcement by a player. The voiced word shows that the player believes themselves to be the first person in the Play Vehicle to see a spottable vehicle outside.

Play Vehicle [pley **vee**-i-kuhl]
noun phrase

1. The vehicle containing participating players during the game.

7

Punchee [puhn-chee]
noun

1. A player that receives a punch from a Spotter.

Player [pley-er]
noun

1. A person who willing and legally participates in the game of Spotto.

(All people in the vehicle are referred to as passengers until gameplay begins.)

Spot [spot]
verb

spotted, spotting

1. To observe, detect, recognise, perceive, identify or notice by seeing a spottable vehicle during the game.

   Nice spot, mate.

   I spotted that first.

   Good spotting, Robbo.

noun (redundant)

The Spottable vehicle sighted by a player.

That spot over there, behind the truck.

A point scored

A spot for that? My spot!

(Modern interpretations of the game-lingo has lessened the usage of the word "spot" as a noun. Today you may hear versions of high-Spotto-language being used in phrases such as "Where was that spot, dear son?", or low-spotto-lingo like "I seen somethink like that Spotto before, roit Shazza?")

The word "Spot" as a synonym for points would be considered a more traditionalist use of language. These days phrases like "score a point" and "What's the score" are perfectly acceptable.

Spottosopher [spo-**tos**-uh-fer]
noun

1. a person who offers views or theories on profound questions in ethics, metaphysics, logic and other related fields related to the game of Spotto.
2. a person who establishes the central ideas of some movement, cult, etc.

Spottable [**spot**-uh-buhl]
adjective

1. The state of being fit and suitable for spotting.
2. Being yellow and of appropriate criteria to meet the standards set by the local rules of the game.

Spotter [**spot**-er]

1. Players who have won a round of the game.

   I was the spotter on that one.

The term "Spotter" is now redundant. These days no-one cares if you won the game for a moment because the game has instantly moved on.

Heathens
now refer to yellow vehicles as "Spottoes" instead of "Spots"

Spotkeeper [spot **kee**-puh]
Noun

1. A current passenger of the Play Vehicle who records any points system being used. This person may or may not be included in the game; hence - passenger.

Spot Keepers are now just point-scorers.

As the game of Spotto modernised during the onset of the digital internet age, and the English language began its gooey slip into the quagmire of intellectual history, some of the traditional words and definitions laid out here became either redundant or combined.

Spotter #1

Name: Kiran Woodsking
Moniker: "Carmageddon"
Age: 24
Experience: Novice
Special Skill: Distance

"I love driving west late in the afternoon trying to pick out spottoes in the glare of the sunset. I don't get headaches anymore and my doctor says that those burnt spots on my retina might heal by themselves.

I had to give up on my dream of becoming a pro-spotter but I still enjoy teaching Introductory Spotting at the PCYC. "

The ride starts here. We remind you of everything you need to get familiar with the game. Buckle up!

CHAPTER 1

Folklore

While we usually think of the game Spotto as a children's pastime during long road trips, the game outlined in this book predates cars, or does it? Any quick internet search will immediately show the history of the "Yellow Car Game" tracing its origins to 17th century Britain in the Cotswolds region where the harvest of rapeseed inspires the story as evidenced by Professor J Bulmanovich from the University of South-West Sussex.

Did you know?

The word *yellow* is from the Old English *geolu* or *geolwe*, which is derived from the Proto-Germanic word *gelwaz*.

Rapeseed (*Brassica napus*) was supposedly harvested and then transported to Dublin during an arduous journey of five days, first over unstable cart tracks and then over the Irish Sea. It is said that workers and children would see the empty yellow-stained carts returning from the Bristol docks and they would lightly hit each other on the arm to acknowledge their successful harvest.

The apocryphal teachings continue with lore of George Stephenson entering a new locomotive he called '*Rocket*' into a competition to race from Liverpool to Manchester. Upon departing on his brightly yellow-coloured steam engine, his wife hit him on the arm and shouted "Yellow cart luck!" perhaps to reprise the children's game. Stephenson's *Rocket* was, in fact, a real machine and history shows that the carriage was yellow, but it's the dubious newspaper headline of the day "One Punch Secures Rocket Victory" that really sells the story.

Replica of George Stephenson's Rocket

But guess what? The internet is lying to you – shock horror! Bulmanovich and his university are made up. There is no evidence for either of them anywhere. Rapeseed was never transported at that time because it was worthless and ploughed back into the soil; and the Stephenson's Rocket headline isn't documented anywhere[1].

Most available history of Spotto seems to be smeared into the zeitgeist but not documented anywhere reputably. The best effort was a website registered in 2007, but now defunct, called YellowCarGame.co.uk that claims the title of "Official site of the Yellow Car Game" and the self-proclaimed International Spotto Federation of circa 2019[2]. Unfortunately, most of the self-appointed rule-makers seem to be feeding from the same trough of pseudo-history leading to a perpetuation of misinformation, myths and legend.

The real deal

In 1955, American game designer Henry Hassenfeld of Hasbro fame described a new game called "spot-a-car auto bingo" inspired by a mythical mother who subsituted numbers on bingo cards for makes and colours of automobiles[3].

Most likely the car game Spotto has its Australian origins in free gamecards at BP service stations launched in March[4] 1959. The newspaper ads said "It's NEW! It's FUN!" and by 1960 the word "NEW!" was removed[5].

The BP card is actually titled "Spotto" and resembles Hassenfeld's game but players would attempt to spot items like stop-signs, bridges, caravans etc. The cards were predominantly yellow & green, the colours of BP, British Petroleum.

Why yellow? ●

While the term "Goldilocks Zone" may create confusion or derision, it seems somewhat perfectly apt to describe the occurrence of the colour yellow during our automotive travels. Throughout the years many car colours have become fashionable, some are way too abundant (like black, blue or red) and some are too infrequent (like purple or pink). The colour yellow has found its place in travel-game tradition because it straddles the sweet spot between "Whatever" and "Wait, what?"

Tom Halter, an automotive paint expert, analysed all car colours since the 40s and his article[6] and charts clearly show why yellow is the perfect choice. It is bright, consistent and resists cultish fads like the millennial boom of grey.

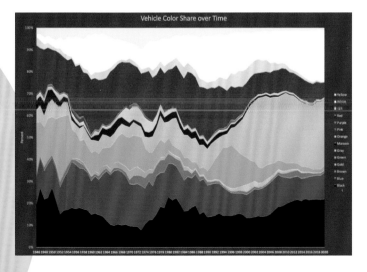

Two games at once?

Why do we punch?

Volkswagen noted that the game of "Slug Bug" was invented by bored American children who would punch each other after seeing a VW Beetle. However their best efforts in researching their own history are no match for the Professor who found an early printed use of the term "Slug Bug" by Mary Jo Bailey in the *Corvallis Gazette-Times*, 21 August 1962, where she described the game.

By 1964 the term was so popular, it was being used in several publications. Even the PR manager of Volkswagen of America, Arthur Railton wrote in to the *Delaware County Daily Times* to comment on the rules[7].

Pinch Mini

The other game played alongside Punch Buggy

Eventually the term morphed into "Punch Buggy [colour], no punchbacks". If little Johnny didn't qualify his victory with "no punchbacks" his sister was authorised to administer retributive violence.

> **Yellow is not an in-between colour, you're either all in or you're not.**
> – Mobolaji Dawodu

Did you know?

Chrome Yellow (lead chromate) was a pigment used for many years from Van Gogh's paintings to school buses – all thanks to French chemist Louis Nicolas

The First VW Beetle was imported into Australia in 1953 by Regent Motors. During the 50s and 60s Beetles were assembled and eventually fully manufactured in Australia. All this ceased in July 1976 as the Bugs could not meet new ADR2&A pollution laws. Since then Beetles have slowly rusted or crashed their way into hens-teeth status on Australian roads.

History shows a correlation between the rise of Spotto in the 1960s, and the advent of the VW Beetle with its own game of "Punch Buggy". Even if the first reports of Slug Bug were in the 60s and 70s there is no doubt the game of "Slug Bug" was imported from the USA smuggled inside the guts of Herbie. So sad however that Punch Buggy has all but rusted to death.

SPOTTO PLAYED AT ANY TIME WITH CARE

Why play car games?

The purpose of car activities on a relatively long trip is primarily to alleviate the tension in the driver, their co-driver (usually the other parent), and lets face it – to:

- get some silence in the car
- distract from fighting
- tire passenger brains to induce sleep.

A well known guessing game is "I Spy" where one player chooses an object in sight and announces to everyone: "I spy with my little eye, something beginning with…" The game is a classic but it has a fatal flaw – it demands attention from the pilot and co-pilot at all times. Why perform a protracted game that involves zero silence and forces parental attention to the max? Car games are supposed to soothe passengers and induce a jolly journey. This game also fills up the airwaves with mindless brain-blurting of guesses and disappointing answers.

Dark yellow? or light orange?

The list of games is long, all the way from 20-questions, licence-plate games, to "name-that-tune". All of the alternatives to Spotto seem to feature incessant noise or stealing solitude from the adults. The answer to this may at first seem easy – colouring books or digital devices. The problem is that these pastimes are "head down" where passengers eyes are not in sync with their head, leading to motion-sickness and smelly cleanups.

KEEPING youngsters quiet and happy while on the road can be done by playing various games. One of the more popular games is auto bingo which keeps all the family occupied so that Dad can drive without distraction—Drawing by F. L. Becerra

"

The colours red, blue and green are real. The colour yellow is a mystical experience shared by everybody.

– Tom Stoppard

Pineapplopia
The mistaken belief that one has spotted a dark yellow car that is, in fact, green

The laziest driver and co-pilot might resort to an unimaginative and timelessly unoriginal game of "who can be quietest the longest". Some go-getters may prepare a printed sheet of things to tick off a list like a scavenger hunt. Tractor… taxi… caravan… cows… ambulance… whatever. You could even be less imaginative and buy it online or get an app. We are approaching the same territory as the original BP cards and preparing your own seems to waste time that could otherwise be spent with a sneaky G&T.

Emotions of yellow?

According to Kendra Cherry[8], MSEd, the colour yellow can have various meanings in different cultures. Most importantly and obvious is that it's attention-grabbing which is why it is always used as the safety colour. While yellow is often a cheerful colour it can also be frustrating, angry or irritating – making it the perfect colour to fill the car-shaped holes in everyone's heart.

Daffodillia

A short term affliction usually aroused during rural trips into the countryside. Sufferers (usually non-gardeners) become aroused at the sight of single yellow flowers or whole fields of yellow crops. The condition is restricted to vegetation. Symptoms subside upon return to urban environments.

CHAPTER

Spotter #2

Name: Finley Falconer
Moniker: "Gold Russian"
Age: 35
Experience: Advanced
Special Skill:
Historic Cars

"I have developed my own patented technique of speed enunciating using a phone app that I made.
I believe in mouth exercises like jaw wiggling, cheek puffing, lip popping and tongue circling.

I hope one day to enter the Guiness Book of World Records for the fastest swiftquip in the cargames category."

Let's get moving.
The engine is running and
it is time for specifics.
Get out your notepad.

gameplay

The finer details and definitions regarding the game may vary by region, or even by family unit. Honestly, it is difficult to track local rules for anyone. However, there is only ONE rule in the game. It is laid out here with many clarifications and discussions to follow in the book.

START SPOTTO

Starting the game

Not everyone has heard of Spotto. It is the duty of every seasoned aficionado to evangelise and teach the ways of Spotto but they must broach the subject carefully. Are you in the same car with the same people you played with yesterday? Okay, sure – go for it. But what happens if you are travelling to a conference with your workmates?

In 1974, after robbing a State Bank of Victoria, a gang of five thieves jumped into the getaway car to evade police. Rumour has it that Carl Gelbman repeatedly failed to start a game of Spotto during the long ride to rural NSW. The money was split four ways.

> **By convention, sweet is sweet, bitter is bitter, hot is hot, cold is cold, colour is colour; but in truth there are only atoms and the void.**
>
> – Democritus (460-370 BCE)

The game may begin in three ways:

1

The game is already on. All passengers have an implied understanding that getting in the car inevitably means Spotto. These players may have previously spotted together or they may have explicitly agreed prior to entering the vehicle.This does not mean the game forcibly remains on. In fact players with this level of telepathy usually have the capacity to switch the game on and off via brainwaves alone.

2

A person may ask the other passengers of the vehicle if they would like to play. Boring? Perhaps. Agreement can be made or a vote may ensue. The peril of embarrassment is always possible for suggesting a travel-game in an unknown setting. The probability of having to explain the game to a newcomer always exists especially when dealing with non-Australians, much like explaining a joke when it's too late.

3

The more traditional commencement of Spotto is for any passenger to simply crown themselves the Spotter (winner) of the round by exclaiming "Spotto" and punching someone if they wish. This is by far the preferred method because fellow passengers are unwitting pawns in the first round that they did not know they were playing. Even if the game is called off by vote or group-shaming, the Spotter still gets a small victory.

Universal Guidelines

Precondition: Players must be travelling in the same vehicle.

Rule: When a player sees a yellow vehicle they proclaim "Spotto!"

(Optional) The winning player may elect to softly punch another passenger.

Must we be inside a car?

Perhaps tradition can get in the way of fun, but it is a car game after all – not a walking game or a water sport. If you would like to play while walking you can go ahead and spot other pedestrians with yellow t-shirts.   You can't play real tennis in the dining room and you can't win the grand final from your Smokey Dawson armchair. If you think you can, then you are just another voyeur or spectator. Either get in the game or stay on the sideline. Spotting cars from the footpath is like describing surfing from an office chair.

Do we all have to play?

Can I opt out? What if the person beside me does not want to play? The game has its emotional roots growing inside the consensus of the group. However if there is a schism or rift the opt-outer is forced to inadvertently imitate a punching bag, bracing for multiple shoulder and leg contusions.

It's all fun and games until someone gets a "sunshiner" or a "lemon lump" and starts looking like they've been in a round with a heavyweight champ. So, play along or prepare to be the group's unofficial bruise collector!

Yellowsa Chromania

Compulsive disorder that causes a person to extend the game of Spotto endlessly beyond the automotive realm. Those who suffer from this condition are known to shout "Spotto" at the sight of a yellow T-shirt or signage. Extreme cases occur when sufferers consider the game "always on" in all circumstances, in abstract forms e.g. spotting in magazines, TV shows or when seeing a bumblebee, corn, butter, sunsets etc. Significant trauma can be caused by repetitive spotting in dreams. Currently untreatable.

1980 Paris Dakar Rally drivers were distracted by the Renault 4 Simpar

Pausing and stopping

The driver has ultimate discretion to abandon the game for themself at any time due to safety concerns. Games are frequently and rightfully stopped while important life-preserving automobile manoeuvring matters are at hand.

Furthermore, the car or school bus may become excessively charged with yellow energy necessitating a pause in the game. This pausability flies in the face of modern players who think that Spotto is "always on" but we must prioritise safety, dignity, and not forcibly keep our offspring in a Spotto-only world – we do need them to grow up just a little bit, but the game will be forever in their hearts.

Many reasons exist for stopping or pausing the game:

- being pulled over by police (aka The "Po-Po")
- listening to your teacher (This will pay off in the long run)
- complicated traffic conditions ("Pipe down for a minute!")

LEFT TURN ON RED PERMITTED AFTER SPOTTING

Geographics

Spotto exists in a traffic universe with many cars around. After all we are trying to perform an eagle-eyed move in the visual chaos of modern traffic. The further we travel out of urban environments into rural areas it follows that traffic decreases and so to does the effectiveness of the game. You may think this induces a major contradiction. Is Spotto a game for suburbia or urbia? Is it short trips or long ones? If we need lots of vehicles around, why play the game when travelling over the Nullarbor Plain?

Saffronym
Severe
Preoccupation
Obsessively
Tracking
Traffic
Objects

Aha! Here lies the eternal beauty of Spotto in all its glory – it requires no preparation, it keeps their little heads up and yes, most importantly, verbal proclamations are infrequent. Silence is golden.

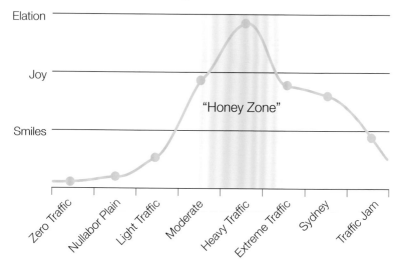

Survey of Spotting Pleasure in Various Traffic

On the school bus

The school bus inevitably descends into a macho game of sanctioned violence. The chaos of a regular school bus contains far too many variables to be accurately examined, so a game of Spotto on a school bus is impossible to imagine. Needless to say the honour-system is abused, and many overzealous fists are thrown.

It is the goal of any Spotto Player to respect their fellow players and err far on the side of pleasant caution, lest the game dissolve into vitriol, bruising and grudges.

The only possible method successfully tested in the wild, to extract a player from a game of School Bus Spotto, is to forcibly remove the Player by using an external force such as a teacher or well-respected colleague not currently involved as an active player. The reason for any one person not removing themselves from the game is due to a certain decline in ego and bus-credentials, or possible excommunication from the clique.

Decree

Players must announce the word "Spotto" loudly enough to be heard by all other players.

The school bus is always a special case. Children are not seat-belted and are free to spin and slide wherever they choose. Punches could come from any direction and lets face it, to any part of the body. Furthermore, the application of rules, guidelines and even personal restraint is such a foreign concept to these developing brains that the big tin box is less of a haven for Spotto and more of a wild west of dread and bruises.

How lovely yellow is! It stands for the sun.

– Vincent van Gogh

In the UK there are no arguments over other types of vehicle. It's so English to shout "yellow car" during a game of Yellow Car when you see a yellow car.

Complexity vs restrictions

Complexity increases as players gain experience and knowledge of the details of concepts outlined in this book. Beginners, usually children, play the simplest form of the game with a wide-open rule set. All yellow vehicles are allowed i.e. spottable. This includes trucks and buses, and for the infants it may include heavy machinery.

The first sign of a novice progressing to the next level is when they display a wilful disregard for the basics. While this generally occurs in the first session, assuming it is long enough, slow learners may require multiple trips to gain experience. For example, they may perform a "Ghost Spot" pretending to see a spot that in fact did not exist (seasoned players are able to take into account other players' body language and head & eye movement etc to determine if a spot was probable even if it was unseen to others.

Worldwide Car-based Arguments Over The Years

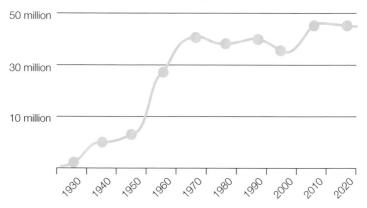

Etiquette

Winning Spotters may wish to clarify the direction and type of vehicle over which they claim the Spot. For example, if a spottable vehicle travels directly in front of the Play Vehicle, a player can declare

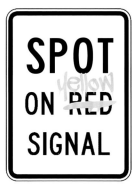

Spotto without noting where the spotted vehicle is. Of course this is due to the lack of ambiguity regarding the existence of a spottable vehicle. However, if a player believes they have seen a spottable vehicle far in the distance, they may proclaim Spotto and swiftly clarify the direction and/or type of Spot. For example, "Spotto, up there, coming towards us". This type of disambiguation by Spotters helps to quickly quash any disputes over the Spot and it also serves to progress the game quickly.

Fallacy or veracity

The game is "always ON" (or is it?)

Are you travelling with your boss? Co-workers? Are we lawyers going to criminal trial? The notion that anyone can, at any time, proclaim to start a car game and then punch, however lightly, their teacher or chauffeur seems ridiculous. Are we to cast aside social graces and appropriate conduct for the assumption that a car game takes precedence over social normality and quite possibly safety? Maybe. Not every occasion is a time to play Spotto, or is it?

Are we supposed to believe that two police officers are using their super-perception powers for spotting only the yellow ones? I like to think so, but bad guys need catching. If the Dakar Rally drivers spent two weeks in the desert dunes playing Spotto we might have a few more accidents.

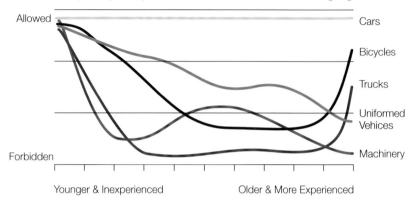

Frequency of Spottable Vehicles with Increasing Age

Allowed — Cars
Bicycles
Trucks
Uniformed Vehices
Forbidden — Machinery

Younger & Inexperienced   Older & More Experienced

What is a spottable vehicle? ⬤

The vehicle spotted by players must be undoubtedly and primarily yellow. Does this mean 50%? Sort of – but there is a need for disambiguation and reasonable agreement between players for a vehicle to be spottable.

Exactly what constitutes a spottable vehicle is probably the most important topic when developing your local rules for the game. Many carguments are started due to disagreement on the finer points of what exactly constitutes a Spot[9]. The following issues must be cleaned and rinsed before any game of Spotto appears in your vehicle.

Spot location ⬤

No doubt that spottable vehicles must be driving on the road, right? But what if the vehicle is on a trailer? Can it be moving in a driveway? I'm just saying, the odds of seeing a yellow car dangling from a crane may be low, but if I'm low on spotto-cred I'll take what I can get.

Paint coverage

While some variants of the game decree that the spotted vehicle is 100% yellow, this inevitably leads to a series of "thrills then killed", obviously because the car is initially spotted and then tracked for verification. Not much fun if the Spotto Police are needed every time.

Many historical rule sets seem to agree on the premise that a spottable vehicle is at least half-yellow. That's 50% or more. The underlying problem with this simplistic view of colour-balance is that it causes more carguments about "is it, or isn't it?" which delays the game and lowers players' spirits. Furthermore, this forces us to tackle the tricky questions:

- must the 51% yellow be on the front of the vehicle?
- what about fancy paint jobs? Stripes?

These nuances are quite a challenge to unpick. The only real solution is to err on the side of unambiguous yellowness.

What percentage of yellow is this one? Hmm?

Vehicle types

Cars

Of course cars are the mainstay of the game. This is never in question. Later we shall discuss variations but for now, we are all good. This includes utility vehicles, SUVs, sedans, coupes, hatchbacks, hybrids, EVs, convertibles, and all similar variations.

Bicycles

No-one has ever truly entertained this as a formal inclusion in the game. Perhaps a team of elite military trained Spotters may have dabbled with this during sniper training but bicycles would be considered out-of-scope for most players unless partaking in a game of Extreme Spotto.

Motorcycles

Motorcycles are for advanced spotters only. They are only included in modern interpretations, due to the lack of yellow coverage even with completely yellow tank and fenders.

Is it a car?
Panel van?
Combi van?
Minivan?
Limousine?
SUV?
Pickup Truck?
Ute?
Hearse?
(Yes or No)

Vans

When they are small, vans are a type of car, right? The only time vans are contentious is when they get too big or the game forbids cars-in-uniform. Insert a can of worms here to allow for a stoush on the topic.

Trucks and Buses

Childs game = yes. These are the first things to be removed. As spotters become more advanced in their abilities, more vehicle types are jettisoned from the game. We all have to start somewhere.

Spottosis Yellophilia

Hallucinations that one has seen imaginary yellow vehicles. This disorder is most easily distinguished during aircraft flights or marine travel. Unfortunately treatment is limited to antipsychotic remedies or transcranial magnetic stimulation.

Heavy Machinery

Excavators, really? Even children could figure this one out with little explanation. Tonka-type vehicles are for toddlers only.

Uniformed Vehicles

Excluding these from the game may increase quality while still allowing players to feel a small rush of exhilaration. False positives still add enjoyment but before you get cocky – define the term "uniform". Go on, then! What about the Uber with that crumpled paper blu-tacked to the back window?

Uniformed vehicle? Does it really matter?

> **Yellow is vagueness and luminousness, both.**
>
> – Vincent van Gogh

Spotto this way, but not that way

Parked cars

Some traditionalists (or are they modernists?) do not permit parked vehicles to be included as spottable vehicles. However the modern game does include parked cars, vans and even trucks, especially for the younger players. But what actually constitutes parking? Obviously we can't tell the exact moment the engine is switched on/off, unless you have infrared vision to see the heat coming from the exhaust. So, is it:

- when the car starts moving?
- when the driver closes the door?
- when they open the door to get in?

Some people may say that any car that is stationary on the roadside is a parked car. But what if they are dropping off a passenger? They have not parked, they have simply stopped during a trip in the same way we all stop at say, a pedestrian crossing. They are still in-traffic.

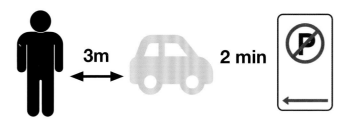

In a No Parking zone, a car is not parked until 2 minutes go by or the driver moves 3m from the car. However, in a car park, time limits and distance do not apply. Stopped = parked.

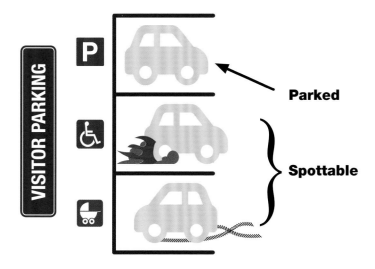

For the ultra-serious diehard stickler who does not permit parked cars consider the following scenario: A perfect Spot is parked in our street. The driver opens the door, gets in, shuts the door and drives away. Essentially the car has gone from:
1. The state of being parked to 2. Being spottable. The same later happens in reverse.

Traditional vs modern

The nuance and difference between regional variation and local rules are impossible to track. Later we shall discuss how the basic rule(s) can be used and extended to create a masterpiece of in-car joy during an otherwise mundane and lifeless trip in the car.

In its purest form Spotto is a game for seeing cars, from within a car. The traditional game of Spotto is played without tally and therefore does not require a points system.

As history progressed and the fashion of paint colours changed, so too did the frequency of yellow vehicles. Government fleets began to use yellow due to its visibility from a distance and its glaring beauty. Therefore, in the modern game, "uniformed" vehicles suffered a decline in being classed as spottable vehicles. This included any small van or vehicle being used for business as evidenced by obvious signage or the presence of tools. Trucks suffered the same fate as they were too easily seen even for the children's version of the game.

Four Types of Spotto Players and Sub-cultures

The diagram on the right shows how one's choice of the two binary tenets can precipitate a quadrant of player types. A third dimension is possible i.e. cars-only vs other vehicles, but this greatly increases the complexity. This has led to street lingo such as "I'm an O.P. Tarmacker" or "Call me a Closed Honeynut".

What counts as a unifiorm?

Settling disputes

Sometimes players will shout Spotto at similar times. The player who concludes their verbal enunciation of the word Spotto shall be deemed the Spot winner. Therefore players have an incentive to complete their enunciation very quickly in order to continue gameplay as a rapid pace.

If there is no clear Spotter, or a player enters an official protestation regarding the validity of a spot, the decision will be adjudicated by consensus among the remaining players in the Play Vehicle, usually by Scissors-Paper-Rock (aka RPS, PSR, Roshambo). If there is no clear outcome, the "carbitrator" shall be the driver of the Play Vehicle.

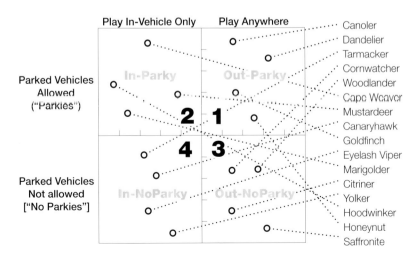

Driving trips

If you have heard of the rule "Shotgun!" with respect to drives, you will remember that this announcement informs other passengers that "I get to travel in the front seat". This edict is generally made when pedestrians (who are soon to be passengers) are in a line-of-sight of the vehicle. While this topic is large enough for its own book, it inspires further investigation.

Starts and Stops

When are you legally allowed to begin spotting? And when is it too late?

Some people might say that Spotto can begin if we are all standing around the car waiting to get in. But if Spotto is a car game it stands to reason that all players must be inside the vehicle. But exactly how far? Is it when the doors open? No-one is in the car yet, so no. Is it when everyone is seated? Maybe. Is it when all doors are closed? Probably. Is it when the engine starts? Surely? Is it when the car is in motion? Definitely.

What if the engine is turned on before the doors closed? These are all pretty pointy things to consider about when to blow the whistle to officially allow play to begin. The only remaining place to draw the line is right next to the motion of the car. Are you allowed to play spotto in a stationary vehicle? If there is such a thing as a Spotto-crime it is playing from within a parked car. This crime becomes more aggravated and harsher penalties apply as player get further from the car.

Splitting

The game is usually played on longer drives during a holiday when boredom sets in, or when restless passengers need to unwind. Let's face it – it's a game derived from parents feebly attempting to keep backseat adversaries alive on the highway without Mum having to take her shoe off and perform a yoga move with evenly distributed violence. For these long and arduous drives there is no need to over think it: we travelled for hours, we had a holiday, and we came home again – that's two separate chances to play two games of Spotto. Here we find the delineation – it is one holiday that includes two main car trips – one there and one back.

But what happens as the travel time and stopover time shortens? Let's explore.

2017 Ruf CTR Yellowbird

41

Overnights

Any overnight stay – that's a no brainer. It's two trips, two Spotto sessions and two chances to thump that person back. Okay, cool. But what happens within a single day?

Long Drive / Long Stop

Everyone gets up early, travels for hours and stops at the friends/in-laws house for a lunch long enough to fry your brain. Then we travel home. Two trips? Two Spotto sessions? Probably.

Short Drive / Long Stop

We embark on a quick drive with the family for a long lunch at a friend's house. It's probably the same scenario as above. Drive-eat-drive. It seems pointless to argue about two chances for Spotto when a large time lapse occurs between them.

Long Drive / Short Stop

What happens if you drive for a long time but stop for a short time? For example, refuelling your dad's Ferrari 250 GTO while on the way to your holiday house in the Byron hinterland? Do you get a second chance to snag that spotto you passed 15 kilometres ago?

Short Drive / Short Stop

Similar to the previous example. We are beginning to see that the length of drive is not our main concern even though it contains all our spotting pleasure. The question is "When does a driving session begin and end?" In other words, what causes the drive to split, and can we double our Spotto pleasure?

More than likely we all agree that Spotto sessions can range from a one-minute drive to 24 hours of Le Mans. The most important question is "When can I legally grab that spot a second time?"

1968 Holden Monaro GTS 327 Bathurst winner

Hacking the system

Once we understand the nuance of driving and after we define our own rules regarding "What constitutes a start and stop" or "Did we start another drive?", we can see how the cunning player may game the system to sneakily steal a few extra Spots. For example: turning off the car at a red light. Does this mean you can spot that car again?

Getting out of the car unnecessarily – are we now on a second leg of the trip, double-dipping on a spot we just made?

If a pizza delivery driver stops in your driveway with the engine running and the door still open, is it another solo Spotto session on the way back?

If you drive a friend home and drop them off in the street, is it one trip or two?

If you are watching the 1968 Bathurst 500 and Bruce McPhee wins the checkered flag in a Yellow Monaro have you just shouted "Spotto!" after each lap, 130 times?

Punching ●

While the traditional game of Spotto rarely exists without an obligatory punch to the arm of the nearest rival, there is a case to be made for its impracticality or even its improbability on anything except a school bus. Looky here:

Driver

The game is Australian so we can dispense with any idea about left-hand drive vehicles. There is really no way that the driver will ever punch with their right hand while maintaining adequate control of the steering wheel. This leaves most of them at a distinct disadvantage, coupled with the fact that they must keep their eyes and mind on controlling the vehicle and they do not have the opportunity to freely scan deeply into side streets. They do however have the rearview mirrors aligned in their favour and can see potential spots behind them.

Consider a taxi driver and passenger who have consented to a game. There are two Players in the Play Vehicle – one in the driver's seat and one player in the back. The backseat player, even with their limited visibility, is easily able to reach and therefore easily punch the driver after scoring a Spot. The problem arises with the driver's inability to effectively punch the back seat player, especially while driving. Is it an underhanded rap with the knuckles? Maybe a hammerfist from over the top?

Now consider the unscrupulous backseat player who decides to slide over directly behind the driver while play continues. That's a power-move.

Disclaimer

The Author does NOT endorse physical violence in any form including jabs, knuckle sandwiches, love-taps, whacks, clobbers or thumps etc. All players must play playfully. Remember, it's all fun and games up to the point of bruising.

Guide

Winning Spotters may exercise their own discretion as to the administration of a punch.

Front Passenger Seat

In a regular car full of passengers the front passenger is at a similar disadvantage to the driver. They cannot effectively use their left hand – it is too far to effectively reach across their midline and strike the driver's left arm, and they cannot squeeze their left arm between the door and the seat to get anywhere close to the rear-seat player. The only left-handed option is to scooch toward the window, spin around and do a little twisting weak punch on the driver's left arm. Not practical at all, but still a better option than doing a full "twist & contort" in the hope of reaching any shoulder in the rear. Most likely the front player will attempt a right-handed kung fu backfist to the driver's left arm. [Note – the driver does not have this ability to do a "scooch and twist" if they are driving safely].

Does Bumblebee only count sometimes?

45

From the Back Seat

Imagine sitting in the back seat of a car. You are in the rear-left and the car is full, seatbelts on, legs rubbing, shoulders bumping. You see a yellow car. What do you do? Shout "Spotto" of course. Now what? You attempt to administer a punch to your nearest adversary.

How do you punch them? Do you use your left hand to reach across your body and then squeeze your fist between the shoulders of you and the other player? Perhaps hitting them in the left of their chest. Even the average person would have anatomical difficulty reaching across their own chest to bury a quick jab in the shoulder of the other player. This assumes that they haven't accidentally provided a glancing blow to their own shoulder in the process.

Do you use your right hand to punch them? How that would work? Do you spin your right arm up and back attempting to "backfist" them in their left shoulder? This feat would require immense flexibility and potential damage to your own rotator cuff. When the middle seat is vacant and a rear-window Spotter wishes to punch the other rear-window player, they must perform a "scoochy twisty", or some variant of a full-arm backhanded, wrist-cocked motion. This means they are more likely to choose to punch front seat players.

Greatest of All Time
Mad Max's Interceptor
New York taxis
Cruz Ramirez from the movie Cars
Ruf CTR Yellowbird
Cheech & Chong's Nash Bridges 1971 Plymouth Hemi Cuda
Bumblebee from the movie Transformers

From the Middle

If the player in the middle seat of a vehicle wins a Spot, they may elect to punch either person next to them (left or right), or in front if the seating plan allows. They may alternate between punchees or continue pounding on the same person. The middle seat player is the only player in the rear of a full car who can effectively punch someone in the arm (the front players). Otherwise they are risking the same shoulder injuries when reaching the rear-window players.

They do have limited lateral visibility but the middle seat position is the chess-queen of Spotto punching.

Statistical Probability and Directionality of Punching

Analysis of full 5-seat car.

Notice how the rear-centre (yellow) has much larger choice. Also, the driver has less effectiveness compared to front-left due to driving responsibilities. Rear-right is greater than rear-left due to most people being right-handed.

Full academic paper available at: www.spottogame.com.au

The case for leg punching

The previous section suggests that arm punching is impractical and could lead to a shoulder injury of the puncher. If leg punching is permitted, drivers can use their left hand most effectively, especially if it is perched in a locked-and-loaded position atop the gear stick, ready to drop onto the player's right thigh.

The opposite is true for front passengers who are at a disadvantage regarding leg punching. In most cases they must raise their right fist up and over the gear stick, and back down to the driver's thigh.

The practical probability of front players performing either an arm or leg punch means that the choice is simply up to them and their own preference.

All back seat players have increased punch-ease and less shoulder hyperextension when using leg punches. This leads the back-middle seat player to now become the Swiss-army knife of Spotto.

Spottatrophy
Sore eyes and facial muscle weakness due to excessive spotting. This occurs with enthusiastic or inexperienced players after rounds of competitive Spotto.

Be wary of wrist and shoulder injuries

Punching early

Punches are only allowed after a player has claimed a verbal spotto. If a spot winner receives an ill-gotten punch from an overeager player who gets a little punchy before their mouth kicks into action, they may elect to punch the other player back twice – once to balance the ill-received punch, and again to claim dominance for the true Spot. If neither of the punchers won the Spot, then a single punch in balanced retribution shall suffice.

Punches are a wakeup call to assert dominance. They are not intended to cause harm.

colour theory

Spotter #3

Name: Torania Leyland

Moniker: "Sunderstorm"

Age: 59

Experience: Intermediate

Special Skill: Cross streets

"I like to scan deep into sidestreets because I know the driver is fixated on nearby traffic and they probably don't use the extended visual reach that I have.

I use a rigorous training technique – I strengthen my shoulders with 3 sets of backfist punching the heavy bag until failure, followed by severe neck hyperextension. My gym buddies called me 'The Owl'."

Is yellow in the paint?
Is it in your eyes?
Is it in your head?
Is it in the universe?
Incoming nerd alert

3
CHAPTER

The human eye

Most people are tri-chromatic. We see using 3 special cells in the back of our eyes called red, green and blue "cones". They send signals to the brain which are processed into a mental awareness of what you're seeing.

Light comes in from the sun and light sources like LEDs or light bulbs. It then bounces all over the place and physical objects absorb some of it, leaving the rest to bounce into the back of our eye.

The misconception is that an object will absorb all wavelengths of light other than the perfect yellow which we see. In reality when we look at a yellow car we are seeing all wavelengths of the spectrum with some being more

Xanthopsia

A real colour vision deficiency in which there is a dominantly yellow bias in vision due to a yellowing of the optical media of the eye

dominant. The yellow paint absorbs some light and then reflects a bunch of wavelengths of photons. Our eyes and brain team up to interpret the light's whole distribution or balance of wavelengths which gives rise to our perception of the colour.

Both cars are the same colour

What is the colour yellow?

Yellow is the colour between green and orange on the light spectrum. It occurs in a dominant wavelength of 570-590 nm. Although the colour yellow as a secondary can be found in emissive colour settings like RGB computer screens, this book focuses on yellow as a primary colour in subtractive colour systems like paint – in particular vehicle painting.

Misconception

False – Yellow cars reflect only yellow wavelengths of light into our eye.

True - Yellow cars reflect a distribution of ALL wavelengths into our eyes.

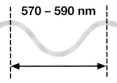

570 – 590 nm

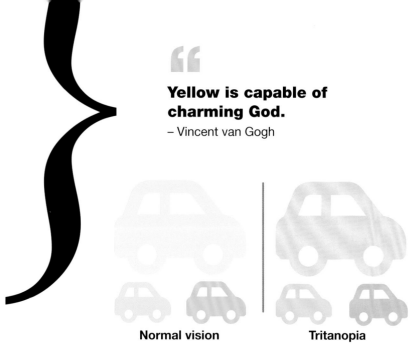

> **Yellow is capable of charming God.**
>
> – Vincent van Gogh

Normal vision   **Tritanopia**

Left: Spotting with trichromacy. Right: Same cars with colourblindness

We see with our brain, not our eyes

While it does seem that wavelengths of light are the same as the length of a piece of string, colour is really a perception – a sensation generated inside our noodle noggins in response to signals coming from the eyes. Colour is not a property of the outside world in the way that, for example, length is.

You've probably heard of colour blindness, a condition where someone will have a anomalous trichromacy (one of their cones is faulty), dichromacy (they only have 2 working cones), or monochromic (they only see in grey scale). Different types of colourblindness have varying impacts for discerning the colour yellow like tritanopia where a person cannot distinguish between blue and yellow colours.

This subject is well documented and complex enough for a series of books but here we will only consider a simple thought experiment.

Imagine a happy couple, standing next to each other, looking at a brand new yellow paint job on a 1978 VB Commodore. One of them is blue-yellow colourblind (probably the genetically-challenged man). They both have the exact same light going into their eyes but if the man has tritanopia the car might appear pale pink, while the other person perceives the car in all its glorious spottability.

Worth noting is that colour blindness may cause a person to miss out on spotting a car, with yellows being diminished in saturation, being perceived as a different colour, or disappearing entirely. Poor, poor chromatically challenged people who may never experience the joys of the game.

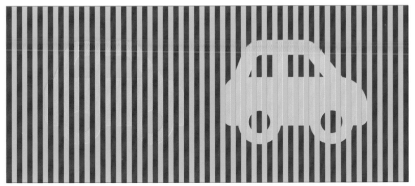

Both cars are the same colour yellow. Yes they are.

YOUR SPOT RISK TODAY IS

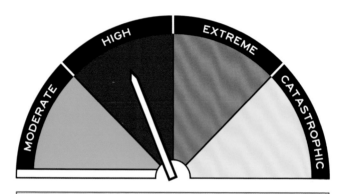

MODERATE HIGH EXTREME CATASTROPHIC

BE READY TO SPOT

SPOT RESTRICTIONS ARE IN FORCE

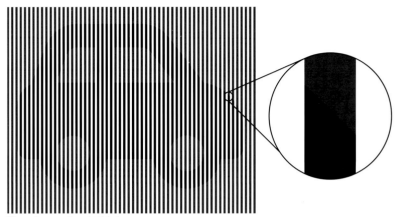

There is no yellow in this image

When is yellow?

Is it a yellowy-orange or an orangey-yellow? Is it lime green or greenish-yellow. The last term in the phrase is the criteria that holds the most weight. A "greeny-yellow" is still yellow by definition.

If we see a yellow car on a black background, it appears darker than if it were on a white background; and even stranger things start to happen when other colours like blue are used. All spotting is done in context with the surroundings. This raises an interesting question: if a car is spotted while parked in front of a blue truck could it become non-spottable in front of a green truck?

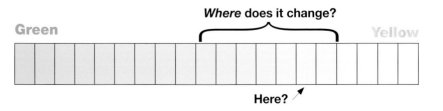

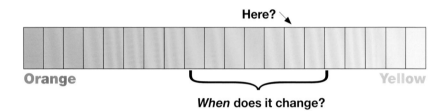

KEEP LEFT
UNLESS
SPOTTING

Here? ↘

Orange   Yellow

When does it change?

Super spotters ●

A small set of the population have a fourth type of cone in their eyes which is most sensitive in the yellow-green part of the visible spectrum allowing them to see 100 million colours. These people are called "tetrachromats". Maybe 12% of women[11] have these special colour-sensing abilities because the genes for this are on the X chromosome and they are more likely to inherit a mutation.

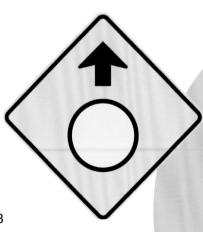

Dark yellow is green

Adding more and more black to pure yellow causes the feeble melon on top of your shoulders to perceive it as green. The only way to trick us into believing in dark yellow is to add a dash of red (or magenta) but after a while it goes rusty orange brown. Yellow is the brightest colour hiding away in the smallest corner of the spectrum.

It starts with pure yellow and only adds black

Mellow Yellow Meltdown
Emotional breakdown triggered by the inability to find any yellow cars during a game of Spotto. This affliction most often occurs in younger players with short-lived bouts of whining and/or listlessness. Treatment involves Temper Tantrum Training [also known as Buttercupset].

Is gold yellow?

Armchair experts in the modern era of the game definitely agree (or perhaps they have all plagiarised themselves) that gold is not yellow even while they provide links to articles contradicting themselves, all while getting quite snarky. The true answer is more complicated.

Sometimes gold is yellow. Sometimes it is not

The pure metal gold is undoubtedly yellow with a metallic appearance. The problem is that the word *gold* is a vague description without any specific reference to colour. Jewellers have co-opted the term to mean any myriad of metallurgic concoctions with only a tiny bit of real gold. Mix in some nickel, palladium or zinc (all of which are "silvery") and voila! White gold! See – it's all in the description and made up language.

So maybe there is no such thing as a gold car, unless you are Sheik Turki Bin Abdullah cruising around like a sardine inside his gold-plated Lamborghini Aventador.

Yellow-coloured objects appear to be gold.

– Aristotle

Modern Paint

1. Pigment (the coloured stuff)
2. Binder (the sticky stuff)
3. Carrier (it dries out later)

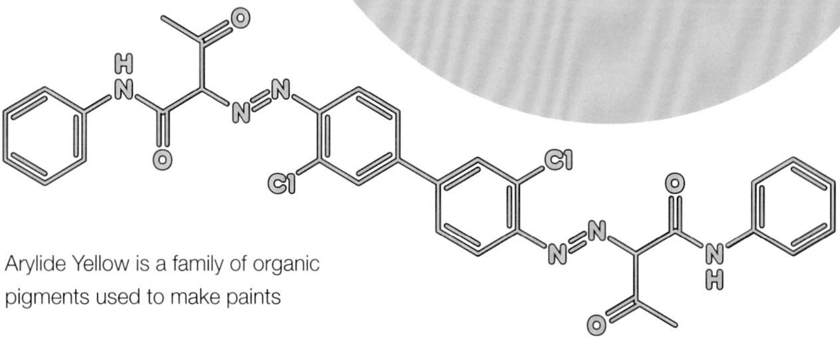

Arylide Yellow is a family of organic pigments used to make paints

Automotive paint history

The earliest cars were hand-painted until the early 1900s when Dr George Seargent kicked off electroplating with chrome. In the 1920s Ford Motor Company began using nitrocellulose lacquers and by the 1930s everyone was doing smooth and vibrant spray-on finishes. Go guys!

The rise of Spotto somewhere in the 60s coincidentally aligns with the dawn of baked enamel finishes leading to durable paint-jobs with more shine which were used up until the 1970s when polyurethane took over.

Hornets Nest

Metallic paint has tiny pieces of aluminium mixed into the paint. What does this mean? Is it metallic yellow? Is it silvery yellow? is it now gold?

[insert cargument here]

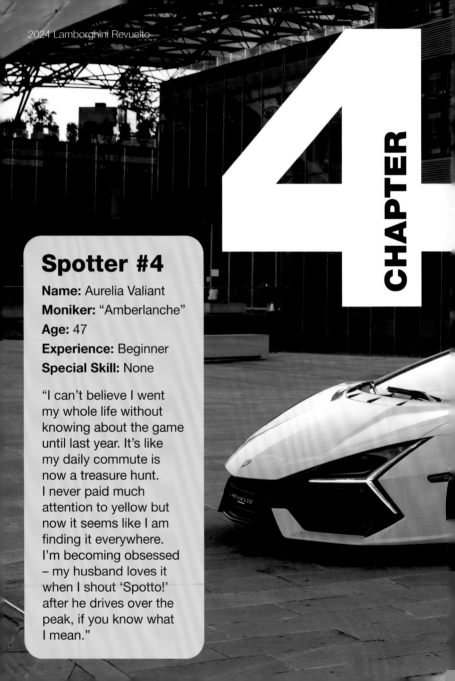

4

CHAPTER

Spotter #4

Name: Aurelia Valiant
Moniker: "Amberlanche"
Age: 47
Experience: Beginner
Special Skill: None

"I can't believe I went my whole life without knowing about the game until last year. It's like my daily commute is now a treasure hunt. I never paid much attention to yellow but now it seems like I am finding it everywhere. I'm becoming obsessed – my husband loves it when I shout 'Spotto!' after he drives over the peak, if you know what I mean."

modern times

**Get with the times.
The times they are a changin'.
Dont get stuck in traffic.**

Digital age

The game was being played across Australia before anyone had a microwave oven in their house, and no-one carried the complete history of mankind in their pocket, so its easy to see that the average person's attention was easy to capture. Since the good ole days when the supply of dopamine outweighed the demand, people have stretched the game more to fit within the digital age. Some have even performed a frankenstein surgery on the game, bolting on bits and pieces in the feeble attempt to spawn a new variant.

Spotting early

Some children play Spotto on the school bus with wild and new variations. Reasoning why young boys would relish the chance to modify the game and punch each other without retribution is an hypothesis for another book but the variation is thus:

1. Players gamble that a spottable vehicle will be seen around the next obstacle e.g. corner or building.
2. They preemptively yell "Spotto" and apply an exuberant punch without spotting anything.
3. The Play Vehicle approaches the place nominated by the player.
4. A Spot is either accepted (because it has already been said and punched) or must be retracted.

Cheese Squeeze
Some intrepid gamers have attempted to fork the game into a new name with similar rules, only this time you can slowly pinch the other player.

Silent spotto

Consenting adults with a mutual admiration and respect for the game may enter into a game of silent Spotto, also known as Transcendental Spotto. Rules are the same as whatever have been previously agreed with relation to local laws and etiquette. However the word Spotto no longer requires proclamation. It is implied in the punch.

Players of this version of the game usually have a long history of playing together and rarely, if ever, dispute spots, hence their ability to calmly accept arbitration through mental telepathy alone.

This version is considered advanced and is usually not substituted during a regular game if novices are in the vehicle.

Lonesome spotto

Judgement cannot be passed if no-one else is with you. While the Japanese proverb asks: "If a tree falls in a forest and no one is around to hear it, does it make a sound?", the Spotto proverb asks: "If a lone Spotter Spots a Spot, does it count as Spotto/Spot? The answer is yes, but if a regular game is played for points against points, or Spots vs Spots, the end result is purely hypothetical with winners and losers being one and the same person. Do you punch yourself? In the leg? Bearing this in mind Lonesome spotto is considered a training exercise, not an official game.

Only the sick and unhinged play in New York

Points systems

Traditionally the game is played from spot to spot, resetting after every sighting or after the punch. However some local rules inject a 1-up-1-down system for winning or mistaken spots. This is fraught with corruption when little minds in a full car either forget to monitor the scores of all other players, or they sneak in phantom points for themselves.

Modern times call for digital solutions to problems that previously didn't exist. If a majority of people are addicted to their phone then dumb evolution kicks in to make us more reliant on the supercomputers in our pockets to keep score. Unfortunately there is always an app for that.

Doubles, triples and beyond

Have you spotted two simultaneous spots separated in traffic? That's two separate spottoes – one here and one over there. So you shout "Spotto!" each time while to pointing to each instance. But what if the Spots are inline in traffic (one behind the other)? You have just stumbled upon one of the hidden gems of the game – Conjoined Spots. The player makes a single proclamation followed by the appropriate number of punches which can be allocated to multiple punchees if the winner so chooses. Some say "Double/triple Spotto" while others may exert more verbal artistry like "Daisy Chain", "Corn Convoy" or "Cheesey Chaser".

Extending the game can be a national security risk

Clubs and comps

Several local clubs have emerged to champion the traditional ways of the game and more outlaw organisations are appearing underground: The Sunbeamers of Singleton, the Mimosa Marauders of Maitland, and the Cape Mentelle Canaries who gather to dye their hair yellow every autumnal equinox.

While many institutions campaign for the Great Australian game of Spotto to be included as a trial in the Olympic games, it remains a distant vision much like picking out a yellow hatchback at dusk while driving west on the Eyre Highway at 8:45pm on New Year's Eve.

Dilutions

We could insert an entire chapter for each subject. For example, when is it pink? Does off-white count? Is it orange or brown? Here lies a slippery slope of "making up your own stuff". At first it seems like a great idea to keep the little leg-biters busy, but if we cast our memories back to the section on why we play car games in the first place, it is all too apparent that endless chirping and arguing runs against the grain – let's keep the noise down shall we?

Extensions

Can I play Spotto on a train, boat or aeroplane? Sure knock yourself out, go for it. But you might end up looking like a dog with its head hanging out of the vehicle window.

Can I play during a video game? This sounds like inception-level, split-brain awareness.

Can I play at the Hot Wheels Museum? No comment.

If I proclaim "Spotto!" while reading a book, will I be committed to a psychiatric institution? Mmm...

Silence isn't golden. It's yellow.

– Zell Miller

Please Stop...

Pink = Pinko / Flamingo
Green = Snotto / Froggo
Orange = Taco / Nacho
Purple = Play Doh
Gold = Lotto
Black & white = Zebro

Monikers

 Like the stage names for those playing Roller Derby, Spotto names (saffronyms) are becoming a recent trend for the serious players. Younger players often self-ascribe these nicknames but the best pseudonyms are bestowed upon the great champions after years of service to the game.

- Ebony "Bumble Bonnie" Johnson – for spotting over bridges
- Max "Sunfire Slammer" Yewt – pioneer of drag race spotting
- Caprice "Yolkle Yokel" Bowie – aka "The Toothless Spotter"
- Kris "Doc Lemonaniac" Donnelly – the "Yellow Mind Mechanic"

closure

Hopefully we have all arrived at the same ideological conclusion, which is to say there is only one hard rule in the game, and that rule is a single word: "Yellow". Everything else is a guideline, an agreement or a local custom. The true beauty of this timeless Australian game, in contrast to its international equivalents, is the versatility that it has on a regional or even personal level.

The great game simultaneously exists in the metaphorical & literal, the physical & abstract. It is like a magificent tree in full bloom set within a forest rolling through the hills. Although related, no two trees are the same and we cannot predictively define nor compare them. Each ruleset has a unique beauty that is born, grows and adapts to its environment.

When we apply rigorous thought, philosophy and precise language about the game, a deeper beauty emerges from the chaos. We all know that our personal thoughts belong only to the individual, but we can arrive at a shared understanding of the human experience. In the same way, you may have a defined set of rules within your car, and other people may have a radically divergent system but this does not hinder anyone on their own personal journey to yellow enlightenment.

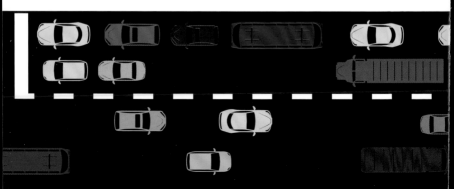

1 joelmorris.substack.com/p/yellow-car-2-the-history-of-the-yellow

2 spottofederation.org

3 *The Tipton Daily Tribune* (Tipton, Indiana) · Thu, Oct 6, 1955, Page 2

4 *The Age* (Melbourne, Victoria, Australia) · Wed, Mar 18, 1959 · Page 19

5 *The Sydney Morning Herald* (Sydney, New South Wales, Australia), Wed, Apr 13, 1960, Page 18

6 https://www.curbsideclassic.com/design-3/curbside-analysis-fade-to-gray-where-have-all-the-car-colors-gone/

7 *Delaware County Daily Times* (Chester, Pennsylvania), Sat, Sep 19, 1964, Page 7

8 https://www.verywellmind.com/the-color-psychology-of-yellow-2795823

9 Stan Tatkin, MFT, PsyD, and founder of the Psychobiological Approach to Couples Therapy Institute.

10 Lardelli-Claret P, De Dios Luna-Del-Castillo J, Juan Jiménez-Moleón J, Femia-Marzo P, Moreno-Abril O, Bueno-Cavanillas A. Does vehicle color influence the risk of being passively involved in a collision? *Epidemiology*. 2002 Nov;13(6):721-4. doi: 10.1097/00001648-200211000-00019. PMID: 12410016.

11 https://jov.arvojournals.org/article.aspx?articleid=2191517

12 *The Age* (Melbourne, Victoria, Australia), Fri, Jan 22, 1965, Page 2

thanks

The Professor would like to thank Cory Spence for providing all of his inspiration, thought, research and good looks for this project.

This masterpiece would not have been possible without the inspiration and graphic genius of the one... the only... Christine Schiedel.

Thoughts and gratitude also go out to Andrew "The Falcon" Swaffer for his foresight and undying loyalty.

index

coming soon

Wheelie Bins

Binjamin Trashington

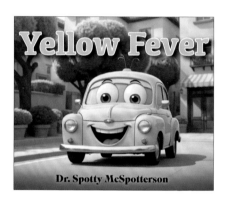

Yellow Fever

Dr. Spotty McSpotterson

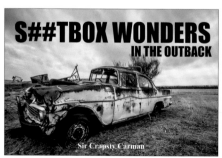

S##TBOX WONDERS
IN THE OUTBACK

Sir Crapsty Carman

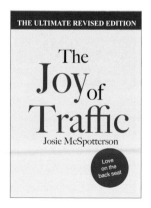

THE ULTIMATE REVISED EDITION

The
Joy of
Traffic

Josie McSpotterson

Love
on the
back seat

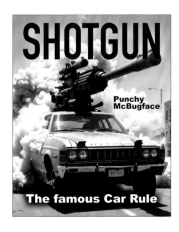

SHOTGUN

Punchy
McBugface

The famous Car Rule

PUNCH BUGGY

Biffy Swingerson

The History of Parentally Sanctioned Violence

Bump & Grind

Smashley Bumpkins

Making and Breaking Children

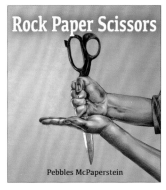

Rock Paper Scissors

Pebbles McPaperstein

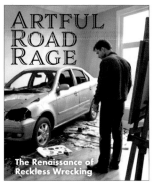

ARTFUL ROAD RAGE

The Renaissance of Reckless Wrecking

Black Holes, Clown Cars & The Infinite Universe

Jester Schwarzschild

credits